Welcome to the laboratory of the world!

Air is all around you! What makes planet Earth so special is that it is wrapped in a layer of air. You can't see it . . . but you can see tall grasses bending as the air moves them, you can feel the wind on your face, you can smell the scents of flowers wafting to you on the breeze.

Imagine a world that had no air. How different everything would be. Nothing could live—no plants, no animals, no people. Air is part of the way the world works, and all living things depend on it.

But *why* is there air? The 'why' questions are always the hardest! The most famous book in the world, the Bible, says that in the beginning, God made the world the way it is as the perfect home for plants and animals, and the people he made to take care of it.

Contents

► 1 Air everywhere

Air is all around you!
You look through air all the time, but you never see it. Air itself doesn't have a special smell, or any taste.

- You can feel air when the wind blows on your face.
- You can hear the noise of air rushing on a windy day.
- You can see things moving in the breeze.
- You can feel your chest getting bigger when you breathe air in, and you can feel the air coming from your nose or mouth when you breathe out.

Air is part of the great design for the world. People, animals and plants all need it in order to live.

God gives life and breath and everything else to people everywhere.

From chapter 17 of the book of Acts in the Bible

The Wonder of Air

by
Bonita Searle-Barnes

Illustrated by Colin Smithson

A LION BOOK
Oxford · Batavia · Sydney

Text by Bonita Searle-Barnes
Copyright © 1993 Lion
Publishing
Illustrations copyright ©
1993 Colin Smithson

Published by
Lion Publishing plc
Sandy Lane West, Oxford,
England
ISBN 0 7459 2023 3
Albatross Books Pty Ltd
PO Box 320, Sutherland,
NSW 2232, Australia
ISBN 0 7324 0506 8

First edition 1993

Acknowledgments

Photographs by The Image
Bank/Joseph Devenney:
spread 9 (bottom); Lion
Publishing/John Williams
Studios: spread 14 (bottom);
Oxford Scientific Films/Mike
Birkhead: spread 14 (top)/
Deni Brown: spread 7/Colin
Milkins: spread 11/Alastair
Shay: spread 9 (top); Zefa
(UK) Ltd: cover, spreads 4,
5, 8

A catalogue record for this
book is available
from the British Library

Printed and bound in
Singapore

Air...
and a whole lot
more!

Children love finding out about the world they live in. This book provides
loads of activities to help them find out about air. They can have hours o
fun watching the way it works and noting their discoveries. In this way the
will learn the basic skills of scientific research.

- *More* They can also find out about some of the ways air can be put
  to work in everyday technology. Exciting projects enable them to
  discover the fun and the satisfaction of inventing.

- *More* Throughout the ages, children, poets, artists, and some of
  the world's greatest scientists have thrilled to the wonder of the
  natural world. The photos in this book are a starting-point for
  discovering more about it. Encourage children to think about the
  different ways they experience air, even though they cannot see it:
  the feeling of the breeze on their faces or in their hair, the sight of
  grasses bending and leaves fluttering, the smells wafted from far
  away on the lightest breath of air... and help them to enjoy their
  world.

- *More* This book helps them, too, to find words that express the
  sense of excitement and joy in it all. Here is an opportunity to
  explore the rich heritage of poems and songs that people have
  written to celebrate their world. For example, this book draws on
  passages of the Bible which have echoed the feelings of millions
  throughout the centuries and which reflect the belief that the
  world is not the result of chance but the work of a wise and loving
  God.

- *More* There is also the question of how the world around us affects
  our feelings. Think of the thrill of holding the string of a kite that dips
  and soars high above the ground; of the sense of mystery as a
  quiet breeze whispers by; the feeling of fear and awe as strong
  winds bend towering trees and send their branches crashing. It is
  a perfect opportunity to talk about such fears, and to offer
  reassurance.

- *More* Going beyond the everyday world, you will find natural
  openings for talking about the symbolic use of air and the wind,
  which they will find in songs and stories and in a good deal of
  religious language. For example, the Bible likens the power of
  God to the wind: it is something you cannot see, although you can
  see what it does. The symbol of wind as an invisible power is found
  in other religions too.

This book is intended to give a very broad approach to exploring the worl
of air that will enrich your children's total understanding of their world. You
be surprised at what you discover, too, as you explore the world through
child's eyes.

Air supply

here are all kinds of wonderful creatures in the world around us.

There are great green caterpillars that munch on leaves, tiny insects with brilliant patterns, slow, slimy snails that slither along ... and many, many more.

- It can be interesting to trap them in a jar so that you can watch them more closely. But remember that living things need air: always make sure you leave an opening so that the creatures can have fresh air to breathe.

- If you need to put a cover on the jar, use a piece of cloth and a piece of elastic. The cloth will let air go through.

- Put the creatures back where you found them after you have enjoyed looking at them for a few minutes.

▶ 2 Hot air

When air gets warm, something special happens to it.

Hot air balloon

You will need a grown-up to be your laboratory assistant for this experiment.

You will need:

- a saucepan
- water
- a glass bottle with a narrow neck
- a balloon

What to do:

1 Pour a little water into the saucepan.

2 Fit the balloon firmly over the neck of the bottle. See how the balloon droops!

3 Now put the bottle in the pan of water. Ask your grown-up assistant to heat the water in the saucepan gently. It will take several minutes to get really hot.

4 Then the water will bubble, the bottle will be hot, and the air in the bottle will get hotter too.

- What happens to the balloon? What is filling it?

When air gets warm, it needs more space.

Because less hot air is needed to fill the space inside the balloon, a balloon of hot air is lighter than the cooler air around. So up it goes!

In the basket is a special fire, to keep the air hot!

Floating balloons

Some balloons are filled with helium. Helium is lighter than the air around us, so they float up on their strings.

They can even carry weights.

- Try putting sticky putty on the string of a helium balloon.
- How well does it float with different amounts of putty?

▶ 3 Wind

Wind is air that is moving. It may be a soft breeze, or a blustery gale.

When a patch of air is warmed by the sun, it rises upwards. Cooler air rushes in to take its place.

But where does it come from? And where does it go? And is it real if you can't see it?

Praise be to God for our brother the wind,
and for air and cloud, still days and storms,
which all things need to stay alive.

Francis of Assisi

Wind watch

- See how many things you can find in this picture that are being blown by the wind.
- Watch how trees and flowers move on a windy day. Do they always move in the same direction?
- Do the trees move as much as the flowers? Why, or why not?
- What does the wind do to your hair? Your clothes?

▶4 Invisible power

A strong wind is an invisible power, moving anything that gets in its way.

A strong wind can be dangerous.

But even strong winds are part of the way the world works, bringing down old trees and sweeping away old, dead leaves.

God is great.
He can do what he wants.
He brings storm clouds, and lightning,
and strong winds.

From Psalm 135 of the Bible

Windbreak

You're outdoors on a windy day.
How can you build shelter from
the wind?

Here are two designs to try:

Which one do you think works best?
Can you use both ideas to make an
even better windbreak?

▶ 5 Wind at work

People have found ways to use the power of the wind to do useful things for them.

People have designed windmill sails to catch the wind so that they blow round and round.

The pole they are attached to also goes round, and can be used like a handle to turn all kinds of machines.

Blow boat

You can make a boat like this from a plastic tub, with a straw for the mast and paper for the sail.

Try blowing it across a bowl of water.

Now try to move it back in the other direction. What do you have to do to make this happen?

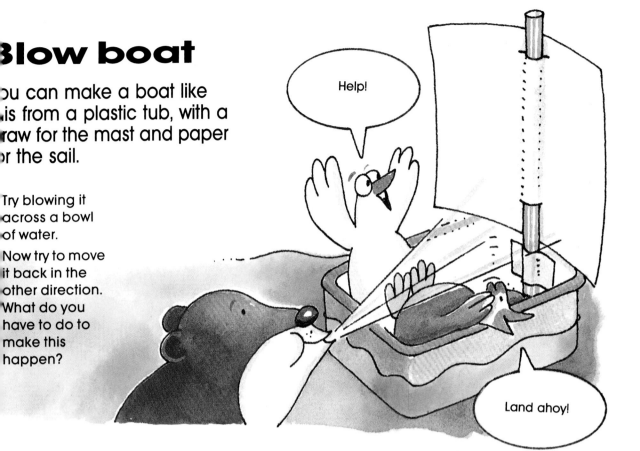

Windsong

Have you ever heard the wind whistling round the rooftops? Have you heard it howling through the trees? When air has to squeeze through a narrow space, you hear the noise it makes.

That's what happens when you whistle!

People can't stop the wind blowing! It is like an invisible power. Jesus, the founder of Christianity, said that the power of God is like that.

*The wind blows wherever it wants.
You hear the sound it makes,
but you do not know where it comes from
or where it is going.*

From the Gospel of John, the book he wrote about Jesus in the Bible

▶ 6 Kites

Wind blows kites high into the air. Make your own kite, and watch it soar.

A simple kite

You will need:

- a piece of plastic cut from a bag, 30 cm by 22 cm
- two paper straws each 21 cm long
- scissors
- sticky tape
- string
- thick needle
- coloured tissue paper or plastic cut from a bag

What to do:

1 Fold the plastic in half along the short side and cut it to shape.

2 Open up the plastic and tape the straws in place.

3 Stick two extra layers of tape on the corners. Now put a piece of string about 50 cm long through the needle and thread it from corner to corner. This is the bridle.

4 Find the centre of the bridle and carefully knot it to make a loop.

5 Tape a piece of string 1 m long from the bottom ends. Knot paper bows along each piece.

6 Now loop a long piece of string to the bridle and knot it.

► 7 Falling through air

Everything that falls has to fall through air. Find out how this affects the way things fall.

A plant makes seeds that will grow into new plants, but how can it sow them?
   Some seeds are designed to float in the lightest breeze, so they can travel long distances. At least some of them will find a place to grow.

These tiny dandelion seeds are attached to a fluffy whorl rather like a parachute.

- If you can find a dandelion head, try blowing the seeds to see how far they travel.
- Nip off one seed, then drop it from the same height as a seed with a parachute.
- Compare how fast they fall.

Whirlybird

You will need:

- a piece of paper 3 cm by 10 cm
- sticky tape
- drinking straw
- sticky putty

What to do:

1 Cut the paper as shown.

2 Cut the straw in half and tape it to the end.

3 Add a small piece of sticky putty to the end of the straw.

4 Throw your whirlybird and watch how it falls.

Parachute

- a piece of plastic cut from a bag, about 40 cm by 40 cm
- 4 pieces of string, each about 30 cm long
- sticky tape
- a small toy

What to do:

First, throw the toy in the air. Watch how it falls.

Tape the pieces of string to each of the four corners of the plastic.

Tie the other ends of the string to the toy.

Go outside and fold the parachute and string in a zig-zag. Throw it high into the air.

Watch the parachute open. Why does it open slowly? What difference does it make to how the toy falls?

▶8 Gliding

Have you ever seen birds drifting lazily in the sky, never flapping their wings?

These birds are gliding. Their wings are designed in a special way to help them float on the air. This way they can watch for the kinds of food they eat in the water, then swoop down to grab it.

Superglider

Take a square of paper, about 20 cm by 20 cm.

Fold it as shown.

Now hold it between your finger and thumb and send it through the air. Does it glide?

Watch the way it moves, and the way it comes in to land.

Try adding a piece of sticky putty or a paper clip to the front of the glider. Does it fly better? Add more weight to the front and see what happens.

▶ 9 Flying!

Many living things can fly. You can't see anything holding up the butterflies that hover above flowers, or the birds that soar in the sky, or the bats that flit through the darkness.

However, air is very powerful. The wings of these creatures move the air in such a way that it holds them up.

Watch the birdie!

Watch birds flying. Watch them flapping, fluttering, gliding, soaring, dipping, diving.
Do they fly through the sky in a straight line? Or do they swoop up and down?

● Draw a line to show the patterns that different birds make.

Brilliant design work in these wings, you know.

A flying lesson

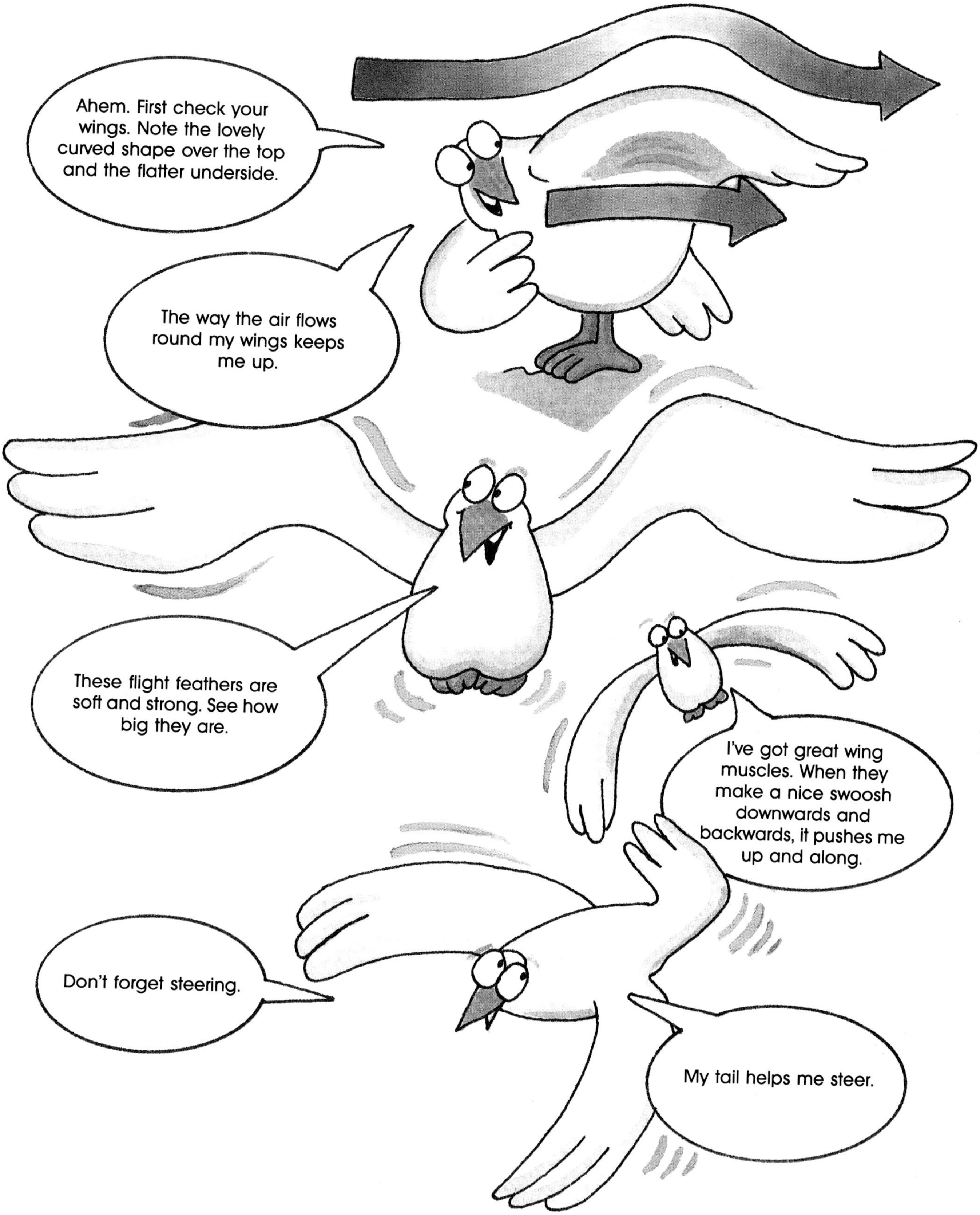

▶ 10 Flying machines

Imagine being able to fly!

People are not designed to fly like birds, but they *are* designed with amazing brains and hands. They are better than any other creature at inventing machines and making them.

They have looked at the brilliant designs of birds in the world around them, and copied the work of the world's Designer.

People have invented aeroplanes to fly in.

Like a bird an aeroplane has to do two things in order to fly.
1.Stay up.
2.Move along.

Lift-off!

The air that travels over the curved top part of a bird's wing travels faster than the air going underneath.

Aeroplane wings are curved on top and flat underneath to make the same thing happen.

Try this experiment to show that when the air blowing over something is going faster than the air under it, you get lift-off!

1 Take a piece of paper, about 3 cm by 30 cm.

2 Hold one short end just under your bottom lip.

3 Blow very hard, so your breath goes fast over the paper. What happens?

et power

et power is one way to move a flying machine forward. Jet aeroplanes take n air in the front of the engine, then queeze it and heat it so that it rushes o escape out the back! This rush of air ackwards moves the plane forward.
You can make a balloon jet.

You will need:

- about 3 metres of smooth string
- a straw
- 2 chairs
- a balloon
- sticky tape

What to do:

1 Thread the string through the straw, then tie each end to a chair. Space them so the string is held out straight.

2 Blow up your balloon, and squeeze the end firmly while someone helps you tape the balloon to the straw.

3 Take the straw to one end, so the open end is next to the chair. Let the balloon go.

4 What pushes the balloon along? How far does it travel?

▶ 11 Floating

Look in a pond, or a fish tank.

Can you see tiny, silvery bubbles floating to the top?

The different plants and animals that live in a pond are cleverly designed so tha they can use the air that is ir the water.

The bubbles you can see are bubbles of air breathed out by the underwater plant and animals. They always float upwards.

Bottle-nosed dolphin

You will need:

- a plastic bottle with a narrow neck and a screw top
- a waterproof pen
- a bowl of water

What to do

1 Draw a dolphir face on the bottle.

2 Take the cap o the bottle and lower the bottle nosed dolphin into the water.

3 Watch the bubbles!

4 Now put the top on your bottle-nosed dolphin.

- Try holding it underwater now. Will it stay there?
- Will it stay underwater if you empty the water out and put the top on

Balloon raft

Your air-filled balloons will float on the water like a raft.

Balloons can burst easily. Don't ever trust them to keep you afloat.

You will need:

- 4–6 sausage-shaped balloons
- string or wool
- two thin sticks

What to do:

1. Blow up the balloons so they are all about the same size. Tie the tops tightly shut.
2. Now tie the sticks to the top and bottom ends of one balloon, crossing the string to hold it firmly.
3. Next, tie the rest of the balloons to the sticks in the same way.
- Try floating the raft in the bath. Give some waterproof toys a ride.

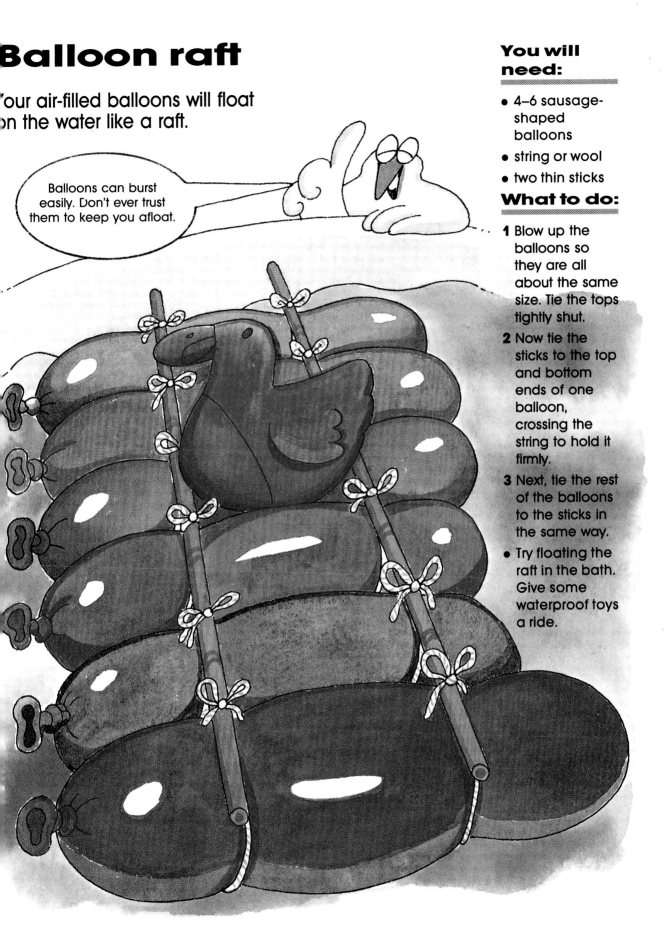

▶ 12 Airless

Air is everywhere!
   If there isn't enough air in one place, more will rush in to fill the empty space.

Drinking machine

Use the laws of science to drink without touching the glass!

You will need:

- a drink in a glass
- a drinking straw

I do enjoy a little scientific research when I'm on holiday.

What to do:

1 Put the straw in the drink.

2 Suck the air out of the straw. What rushes in to fill the space?

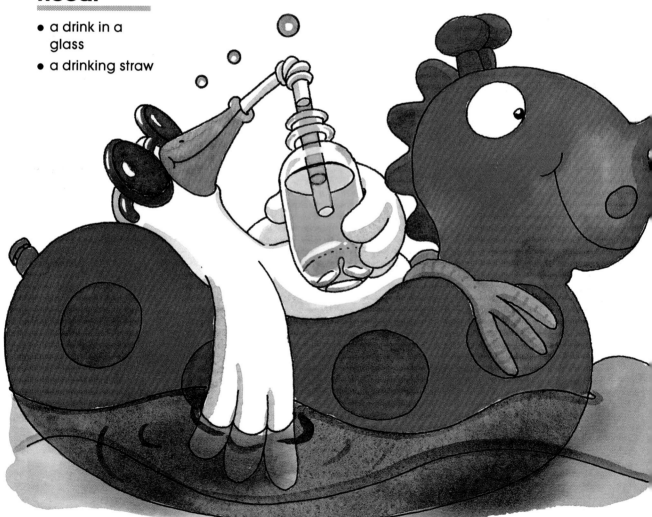

Vacuum cleaner

A space with no air is called a vacuum. A vacuum cleaner has a motor that makes a vacuum near one end of the tube. Air and any loose bits rush in the other end. A clever use of the way air works!

- Try picking up objects on the end of a straw by sucking in.
- Be very careful not to suck on anything so small that it might go up the straw.
- Try a piece of paper, a small sweet, a ping-pong ball.
- Try playing a game with a friend, to see who can pick up things the fastest.

▶ 13 Air transport

Air race

Make the air move for you! Use [it] to race your champion leaf to the winning post!

What to do:

Fold the stiff paper concertina-fashion. Hold one end of the folded paper and fan it out.

Cut two leaf shapes out of the soft paper.

Flap the fan to make the leaf move. Have a leaf race!

▶ 14 Air blankets

Look at this bird! It has fluffed out its feathers so much that it looks a lot bigger than usual.

Of course, it is really still the same size, but there is more air trapped between each of its feathers.

The bird's body warms the air, and its feathers hold this blanket of warm air around it, to keep it extra snug.

Look at this piece of fleece from a sheep's coat. It has lots of spaces to hold the air.

Even when it is made into cloth, wool still has lots of tiny air spaces. That's why it's good at keeping you warm.